W9-BEE-046

iMath
Readers

Picnic Fun:
Hot Dog Operations

by Donna Loughran

Content Consultant
David T. Hughes
Mathematics Curriculum Specialist

NORWOOD HOUSE ■ PRESS
Chicago, IL

Norwood House Press
PO Box 316598
Chicago, IL 60631

For information regarding Norwood House Press, please visit our website at
www.norwoodhousepress.com or call 866-565-2900.

Special thanks to: Heidi Doyle
Production Management: Six Red Marbles
Editors: Linda Bullock and Kendra Muntz
Printed in Heshan City, Guangdong, China. 208N—012013

Library of Congress Cataloging–in-Publication Data

Loughran, Donna, author.

Picnic fun: hot dog operations / by Donna Loughran and Linda Bullock;
consultant David Hughes, mathematics curriculum specialist.
pages cm.—(iMath)

Audience: 6–8
Audience: K to grade 3
Summary: "Addition and subtraction concepts are introduced through a story
about a picnic. Basic addition and subtraction problems are presented as
they are used to help plan the picnic. Different methods of addition and
subtraction are used, such as a ten frame, linking cubes, and counting
on/back. Includes a discover activity, a science connection, and
mathematical vocabulary introduction"—Provided by publisher.

Includes bibliographical references and index.

ISBN: 978-1-59953-548-7 (library edition: alk. paper)
ISBN: 978-1-60357-517-1 (ebook)

1. Addition—Juvenile literature. 2. Subtraction—Juvenile literature.
I. Bullock, Linda, author. II. Title.

QA115.L75 2013
513.2'11—dc23
2012023823

CONTENTS

Note to Caregivers:

Throughout this book, many questions are posed to the reader. Some are open-ended and ask what the reader thinks. Discuss these questions with your child and guide him or her in thinking through the possible answers and outcomes. There are also questions posed which have a specific answer. Encourage your child to read through the text to determine the correct answer. Most importantly, encourage answers grounded in reality while also allowing imaginations to soar. Information to help support you as you share the book with your child is provided in the back in the **Additional Notes** section.

Bold words are defined in the glossary in the back of the book.

Time for a Picnic

It Is a great day for a **neighborhood** picnic. The sun is shining. The weather is warm. There is food for everyone. And there are games to play.

Lots of people are at the picnic. Look at the picture. There are 2 adults and 2 children at the table. How many people are there in all? $2 + 2 = 4$.

Now count the hot dogs on the plate. There are 7 hot dogs in all. If somebody takes 2, how many are left? $7 - 2 = 5$.

In this book, you can join the picnic, too. There, you will think about ways to **add** and **subtract**.

When you put things together, you add. The total is a **sum**.

When you take things away, you subtract. What is left is the **difference**.

How Many Hot Dogs Are There?

Mr. Garcia picks up a pack of hot dogs. Look at the picture. How many hot dogs are there in all?

Mr. Garcia puts four of the hot dogs on the grill. Can you find out how many hot dogs are left?

Idea 1: Use a **ten frame** to add and subtract the hot dogs. Draw one circle for each hot dog.

Cross out four hot dogs. How many are left?

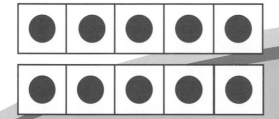

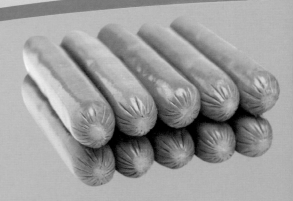

Do you think this is a good way to find the answer?

Why or why not?

Some hot dogs are made of meat. Others are made from soybeans.

Idea 2: Use **linking cubes**. Use one cube for each hot dog. Add cubes to show how many hot dogs there are in all.

Take away cubes to find how many hot dogs are left.

Do you think this is a good way to find the answer? Why or why not?

Idea 3: You can **count on** and **count back**. You count forward to add. You count backward to subtract.
There are 5 hot dogs in one row.

Start at 5 to count on. 5, 6, 7,___,___,___
Count on to count all of the hot dogs.

Mr. Garcia started with 10 hot dogs. He put 4 of the hot dogs on the grill. Count back to find out how many hot dogs are left. 10, 9, 8,___

Do you think this is a good way to find the answer? Why or why not?

Materials
- paper
- pencil
- 2 number cubes
- a set of blocks

Roll Some Numbers

Play a game with a friend or family member. Roll two number cubes. If both numbers are the same, roll again.

Which cube shows a larger number? Count a matching number of blocks.

Which cube shows a smaller number? Take away a matching number of blocks. How many blocks are left?

This is your score.

Now it is your partner's turn.

The first player to get 25 points is the winner.

Find Sums and Differences

There is lots of food at the picnic. There are watermelons and corn. There are bunches of grapes and oranges with thick skin.

Of course, what is a picnic without hot dogs? People put all kinds of things on their hot dogs. Some use ketchup. Others use mustard. People use pickles and onions, too.

There are 4 bottles of ketchup and 8 bottles of mustard on a picnic table. How many bottles are there in all? Use ten frames to add the bottles. The answer is the sum.

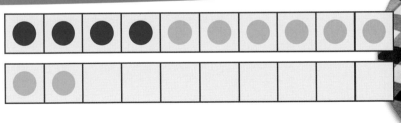

What do you like to put on your hot dogs?

Mr. Stuart takes away 2 ketchup bottles and 3 mustard bottles to fill up again. How many bottles are left on the table? Use the ten frames to subtract. The answer is the difference.

Pickles are a favorite picnic treat. Some are very sour. They make your mouth pucker.

Others are sweet. They are juicy, too.

There are 8 jars of pickles on a picnic table.
Mrs. Little brings 3 more.
How many jars of pickles are there in all?

Use linking cubes to find the sum.

Which do you like better, sweet or sour pickles?

Mr. Jenkins puts 5 of the jars of pickles in an ice chest to keep them cool. How many jars are left on the table? Use your linking cubes to find the difference.

Ooooh! There are chopped onions to put on hot dogs. Onions pick up **chemicals** (KEM-ih-kulz) from the soil in which they grow. When someone cuts the onion's skin, the chemicals enter the air. The air touches your eyes.

Your eyes tell your brain that something is bothering them. Your brain tells your eyes to make tears. The tears wash away the chemicals.

There are 10 bowls of chopped onions on the picnic table. Mr. Diaz brings 5 more bowls.

How many bowls of onions are there in all?

Start with 10. Count on to find the sum.

People use lots of onions on their hot dogs. Soon, 2 bowls are empty. How many bowls are left on the table?

Do you put onions on your hot dogs?

Start with 15. Count back to find the difference.

Order Doesn't Matter

The Garcias are at the picnic. They have 5 people in their family. The Jenkins family is here, too. They have 6 people in their family. So do the Martins. How many family members do these families have in all?

$$5 + 6 + 6 = ?$$

There are other ways to write the problem, too.

The numbers you add are called **addends**. It does not matter what order they are in. The sum is always the same.

$$6 + 6 + 5 = ?$$

$$6 + 5 + 6 = ?$$

These children are identical twins

Mr. and Mrs. Fisher arrive. They bring their twin boys. The boys were born at the same time. They look like both their parents. They also look like each other.

How many people are at the picnic now? Does it matter how you order the addends?

Here's a joke for you. What do you call a group of puppies on a warm day? Hot dogs!

Connecting to Science

Have you ever wondered why children look like their parents?

All living things make more of their own kind. Dogs make more dogs. Butterflies make more butterflies. Oak trees make more oak trees.

Living things that come from other living things are called **offspring**. Dogs have offspring. They are called puppies.

Offspring look like their parents. Do you know about ligers and tigons?

People have crossed lions and tigers to make ligers, like this one. Ligers do not live in the wild.

A liger is the offspring of a male lion and a female tiger. Its fur is orange-brown, like a lion. And it has stripes like a tiger.

A tigon is the offspring of a female lion and a male tiger. It can roar like a lion and growl like a tiger.

What do you think a cross between a zebra and a horse would look like?

Math at Work

Chefs work at restaurants. **Pastry** chefs make **desserts**. They use math in their work. They figure out how many and what kinds of desserts to make. They read their **recipes**.

Recipes list what chefs need to make a dessert. Many desserts have flour, butter, and sugar in them. Recipes also give **measurements**. Measurements tell chefs how much flour, butter, and sugar to use.

Apple pie is a dessert. Many chefs make it. Many families make it, too. In the U.S., people often make apple pie for July 4th picnics!

Lots of Americans eat apple pie at July 4th picnics.

What's the Word?

Have you ever heard the song "The Teddy Bear's Picnic"?

Here are some of the words.

Every teddy bear, that's been good

Is sure of a treat today

There's lots of wonderful

things to eat

And wonderful

games to play

Beneath the trees,

where nobody sees

They'll hide and seek as

long as they please

Today's the day the teddy

bears have their picnic.

What kinds of treats do you enjoy at a picnic?

Perhaps there will be teddy bears at the neighborhood picnic.

But they may not want to share their treats!

Picnic Games

Have you ever been in a sack race? What did you like most about the race?

There are games to play while the hot dogs are on the grill. The first game is a sack race.

There are 9 children who each get into a potato sack. A few minutes later, 3 more children join them. How many children are in the sack race in all?

Racers hop as fast as they can. Some racers stumble. They laugh as they roll on the ground. Only 4 racers reach the finish line. How many children do not reach the finish line?

The egg and spoon race comes next. There are 7 children who each take an egg and a spoon. They practice walking while holding their eggs. It is difficult to keep the eggs in their spoons.

There are 9 grown-ups who also join the game. Each of them gets an egg and a spoon, too. How many eggs do the children and grown-ups have in all?

What do you think would be the most fun part of being in an egg-and-spoon race?

The racers walk as fast as they can. But the eggs roll close to the edge of the spoons. There are 3 children and 2 grown-ups that lose their eggs. How many people are still in the race?

iMath Ideas: Count Those Dogs!

All the games have made people hungry. They line up one-by-one at Mr. Garcia's grill for more hot dogs. Each person in line carries an open hot dog bun. Mr. Garcia looks up. Whew! He hopes he has enough hot dogs.

He puts 7 hot dogs on the grill, and 6 hungry people wait in line. Are there enough hot dogs to feed everyone?

Idea 1: You can use a **ten frame** to add and subtract. But it's hard to draw while you are standing in line.

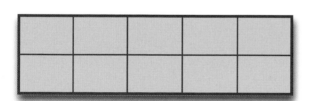

Idea 2: You can use **linking cubes** to find the answer. But you forgot to bring them with you.

Idea 3: You can **count back**. Mr. Garcia put 7 hot dogs on the grill. So start at 7. Then count back.

7, 6, 5, 4,___,___,___.

Are there enough hot dogs for everyone in line? Are any hot dogs left over? How many? It will be good to know how many hot dogs we need for the next picnic!

What Comes Next?

A good picnic takes planning. Plan your own picnic. Ask and answer questions like these:

When will it be?
Where will it be?
Who will come?
What games will you play?

There is another important question. What will you eat? How much food will you need?

Copy the chart below. Then fill in the chart to plan your picnic.

What You Need	How Many You Need
Hot Dogs	
Buns	
Plates	
Napkins	
Ketchup	____ bottle
Mustard	____ bottle
Slices of apple pie	
Blanket	
Teddy bear	

Draw a picture of your picnic basket. Draw more pictures to show who will join you.

A picnic can be great fun!

GLOSSARY

add: to put together; to find how many in all.

addends: the numbers you put together.

chemicals: materials that join to make new materials.

count back: a way to subtract. Start with a number. Then count back by another number.

count on: a way to add. Start with a number. Then count forward by another number.

desserts: sweet dishes.

difference: what you get when you subtract one number from another number.

linking cubes: cubes that snap together.

measurements: the amounts you get when you measure something.

neighborhood: a place within a town or a city where people live.

offspring: living things that come from other living things.

pastry: a sweet baked good.

recipes: instructions with measurements for making food or drink.

subtract: to find a difference.

sum: how many there are in all.

ten frame: a chart for counting on and counting back.

FURTHER READING

FICTION

The Great Adventures of Larriot the Liger, by Megan Meyer, Brosen Books, 2011

The Teddy Bears' Picnic, by Jimmy Kennedy, Aladdin, 2000

NONFICTION

Adding and Subtracting in Math Club, by Amy Rauen, Weekly Reader, 2008

Additional Notes

The page references below provide answers to questions asked throughout the book. Questions whose answers will vary are not addressed.

Pages 6 and 7: There are 10 hot dogs in all. 6 hot dogs are left.

Page 9: There are 12 bottles in all. There are 7 bottles left after Mr. Stuart takes away 5 bottles to fill again.

Page 10: There are 8 + 3 = 11 jars of pickles in all. Mr. Jenkins takes away 5 jars. There are 6 jars left on the table.

Page 11: 10 + 5 = 15; There are 15 bowls of onions. People empty 2 bowls. 15 − 2 = 13; There are 13 bowls of onions left.

Page 12: There are 17 people in all before the Fishers and their twins arrive. Then there are 21 people in all. It does not matter what order the addends are in. 17 + 4 = 4 + 17

Page 14: It would probably look like both a zebra and a horse. So, it may look like a horse with stripes.

Page 17: 9 + 3 = 12 children in the race. 12 − 4 = 8; Eight children do not finish.

Page 18: 7 + 9 = 16 people in the race, so there are 16 eggs in all. 3 + 2 = 5; Five people lose their eggs. 16 − 5 = 11; 11 people are still in the race.

Page 20: Yes, there are enough hot dogs for everyone. There is 1 hot dog left over.

INDEX

Content Consultant

David T. Hughes

David is an experienced mathematics teacher, writer, presenter, and adviser. He serves as a consultant for the Partnership for Assessment of Readiness for College and Careers. David has also worked as the Senior Program Coordinator for the Charles A. Dana Center at The University of Texas at Austin and was an editor and contributor for the *Mathematics Standards in the Classroom* series.

24